PHONES, LIES AND BLOOD LINES

DIVIJA SHEKHAWAT

For every woman who was called crazy for feeling too
deeply,
and for every man who suffered quietly in someone else's
shadow.
May truth always find its way out of the bloodline.

Contents

Contents

FOREWORD

When I first came across the real-life headlines of cold ambition and buried truths in India's elite circles, I was struck not by the crime—but by its silence. The kind of silence that doesn't scream guilt but whispers corruption. This novel is a fictional take, inspired by the undercurrents of inheritance wars, obsessive love, and the manipulation of truth in modern India. Every lie, every phone, and every bloodline in this story speaks to what happens when family becomes battlefield. The funny thing about this story is that it was an actual dream.

    – Divija Shekhawat

PREFACE

Phones, Lies & Bloodlines was born out of a simple yet dangerous question: What if the murderer wasn't the most obvious suspect? In a world increasingly run by screens, secrets don't just hide, they get recorded. This novel explores what happens when power, love, and betrayal are all filtered through the glowing lens of a phone screen.

The chapters ahead navigate obsession, betrayal, and the question of justice in a country where truth can be bought, but never buried forever. I invite you into the streets of Delhi, into the minds of the guilty, and the hearts of the innocent.

Acknowledgements

To my family, who taught me the true weight of silence.

To every journalist, investigator, and writer who digs deep enough to make the world uncomfortable.

To Delhi chaotic, beautiful, cruel.

And to every reader brave enough to fall in love with the villain.

Thank you for stepping into the shadows with me.

PROLOGUE

Ten years after the murder of Arjun Mehta, his name still makes headlines.

Not because of his wealth or the scandal, but because the man jailed for his death—his own cousin—walked out a free man last week.

And someone out there knows the truth.

As I sit with the rusted police files, the contradictory interviews, and a handful of decrypted phone data, I am certain of one thing: the truth was never in the courtroom.

It was always in the phones.

This book is not just a retelling. It is a reopening.

– Dilip Bose, True-Crime Author

From "The Bloodline Betrayal: The Untold Story of Arjun Mehta"

I

Blood on the Marble

The night Arjun Mehta died, Delhi was drowning in monsoon rain.

The downpour beat down on the rooftops of Defense Colony, sweeping away any trace of subtlety from the murder that would change the lives of two sisters, and the city's most powerful family, forever.

Tara Sharma stood barefoot in her living room, rainwater seeping in through a broken window. Her hands were soaked in crimson, and her breaths were shallow. Her mind couldn't compute what her eyes saw: Arjun's body, collapsed awkwardly on the floor of her apartment, his phone shattered beside him, blood seeping into the cracks of the marble floor.

The phone. That damn phone.

The one thing Tara would beg the police to find, without ever knowing it was the one thing her sister Rhea would do anything to hide.

"Ma'am, step back!" The officer's voice barked through the chaos as Inspector Dhritirashtra Rai entered the scene. Impeccably dressed in his brown uniform, eyes sharp under thick brows, Rai moved like a man who'd seen too many dead bodies and trusted none of the living.

Tara's lips trembled. "I didn't... I didn't do this."

"You found him here?" Rai asked.

"I, I was waiting. He said he'd come over," she said, sobbing now. "He never lied about that."

Rai's eyes scanned the apartment: minimalist furniture, abstract paintings, and a framed photo of Tara and Arjun smiling at India Gate. The phone caught his eye.

"Get that bagged," he ordered a constable.

But before they could lift it, another officer called out. "Sir. No SIM card."

Rai's brows narrowed. "Where the hell is the SIM card?"

Across town, in a sleek Noida high-rise, Rhea Sharma stared at her encrypted laptop screen, her jaw clenched. On it was a file directory titled "Distribution_Q4_IllegalAssets.pdf", a smokescreen of weapon deals posing as export shipments. But her eyes weren't on the numbers. They were in the folder Arjun had copied onto his phone. The one she thought she'd deleted.

She had panicked when she heard the news of his death. Not because he was dead, though she'd loved him in her way, but because she didn't know who had his phone.

Beside her, Kanika, her best friend and silent accomplice, lit a cigarette. "You need to move those files again."

"They're already gone," Rhea said.

Kanika looked at her. "Gone like Arjun?"

Rhea shot her a look. "We didn't kill him."

"We didn't. But we were going to blackmail him. That's motive enough."

Back at the apartment, Tara sat on the sofa, wrapped in a police-issued shawl. Her hands trembled as she stared at Arjun's body being taken away.

"He was the only one who ever believed in me," she said softly.

Inspector Rai remained silent, then finally spoke. "Did you know he was sleeping with your sister?"

Tara blinked. "What?"

"You didn't know?"

Her lips parted, but no sound came. Her mind ran in circles, flashes of Rhea smiling a little too brightly when Arjun's name came up. The sudden arguments. The weird silence.

"No," she whispered.

Rai nodded slowly. "We'll be talking again."

Later that night, Rhea stared out her window. Her startup had investors, politicians, and power behind it. But one leak and everything would collapse. She pulled out a second phone, the one she used to communicate with her overseas buyers.

The real phone Arjun had taken was still out there.

And someone, somewhere, had it.

If the police found it, they'd see everything.

So she did what she had to; she called Kanika again. "You know what to do. Hide it where no one finds it."

"I already have," Kanika replied. "You should worry about your sister now. She's too nosy."

"I'll handle her," Rhea said. "She'll destroy herself before anyone else gets to me."

Outside, the monsoon poured.

And a storm much darker had just begun.

II

The Girlfriend Who Waited

Tara hadn't moved from her spot on the old beige sofa in hours.

The apartment still smelled faintly of Arjun's cologne, bergamot, and leather, a scent that clung to the cushions like guilt. The police had left an hour ago, the last of them muttering something about collecting statements later. The chalk outline of Arjun's body still stained the floor, its ghostly presence making it impossible to look away.

Her phone vibrated on the table.

Unknown Number.

She let it ring.

When it stopped, silence returned. Except for the creak of

the fan blades and the buzzing in her ears. She didn't cry anymore. Not since the moment Inspector Rai said the words that sliced through her more cruelly than anything else that night:

"Did you know he was sleeping with your sister?"

Tara didn't believe it. Couldn't. Rhea wasn't capable of something like that, or maybe she was. It had been weeks since Rhea came home late, smelling like smoke and secrets. Tara had convinced herself it was just the stress of her start-up. But now...

Now everything felt suspicious.

She stood up, her knees weak, and walked over to Arjun's phone, the decoy phone, the one the police bagged. The real one was missing, and Tara could sense it. Arjun had two phones. She'd seen them both.

And she knew he had been afraid.

She just hadn't known what of.

Meanwhile, at a posh underground café in South Extension, Rhea stirred her espresso with a practiced stillness that belied the chaos bubbling beneath her skin. Kanika sat across from her, scrolling through her messages.

"The police think Tara did it," Kanika said without looking up.

"Of course they do," Rhea replied. "She's unhinged. Obsessed."

"You do know she might remember the second phone soon."

Rhea blinked slowly. "She won't."

"And if she does?"

"Then she becomes collateral."

Kanika gave her a look. "You sound like your investors."

"I learned from the best."

Inspector Rai sat at his desk that night, reviewing the initial forensics. Time of death: approximately 9:22 PM. Cause: Blunt force trauma to the back of the head. No signs of struggle. No fingerprints on the murder weapon, a heavy crystal vase.

He leaned back, lighting a cigarette even though he wasn't supposed to in the station. Something about Tara didn't sit right. She'd been cooperative, but almost too cooperative. Like someone desperate to convince, not just confess.

But it was Rhea Sharma he had a bigger problem with. On paper, she was golden. A successful businesswoman. Politically connected. But her eyes—they didn't match her smile. And that damn best friend of hers? Too quiet.

Rai picked up his burner and dialed an old contact.

"Ajay. Tech unit. I need you to recover deleted files from a phone we just seized. High profile. Priority one."

Back in her room, Tara dug through drawers and shelves like a woman possessed.

She remembered something, vividly now.

A week ago, Arjun had handed her a tiny piece of paper, folded twice, and told her, "Keep this. Don't open it. Not unless something happens."

She had laughed then. "Why would anything happen?"

But Arjun hadn't laughed back.

She found the note in the back of her journal, buried behind poems and mindless rants.

It read:

"Rhea is hiding something. It's all in the backup folder. If anything happens to me, give this to someone you trust. NOT the police. Not yet."

Tara's hands shook. Her eyes blurred with tears and fury.

She had been waiting for Arjun. Believing in him.

But Rhea?

Her own sister?

Was she the reason Arjun was dead?

By morning, Tara was sitting across from Inspector Rai, staring at him like a woman with nothing left to lose.

"I think my sister killed him," she whispered.

Rai leaned forward. "Why?"

Tara handed him the note.

He read it twice, then looked up. "Did you ever see the second phone?"

She shook her head. "I think Rhea has it. Or Kanika."

Rai stood. "We'll find it. And when we do, someone's going to burn."

Outside, the storm clouds were still thick over Delhi.

And inside a memory card somewhere, the truth waited to be found.

III

Secrets in Her Startup

Rhea Sharma sat in her office with the blinds drawn, the city lights casting vertical bars of shadows across the marble floor. Her start-up, ReNovaTech, was known in the public domain as a logistics optimization company. What people didn't know, what no one could know, was that its actual revenue didn't come from optimization. It came from shipments without invoices, containers without customs records, and names that didn't exist.

Arjun had known. That was the problem.

He hadn't meant to know, not at first. But curiosity had a way of exposing things. One night, while helping Rhea with a software crash, he'd stumbled upon a folder named "ClientDataX." She had told him it was just a dummy test.

Arjun had smiled then, but his eyes had said otherwise.

That smile died the night he copied the folder onto his phone.

Now Rhea couldn't sleep. Her sleekly designed office felt like a glass cage. Kanika stood near the corner, arms crossed, tapping her heel nervously.

"We need to wipe your backups," Kanika said.

"I already did," Rhea lied.

"Rhea, if the police get that phone—"

"They won't. Tara won't let them."

Kanika raised an eyebrow. "You think she's protecting you?"

Rhea paused. "No. But she's too emotional. She'll chase shadows while we burn the real evidence."

Inspector Rai arrived outside ReNovaTech the next morning with a warrant. Flanked by two constables and a digital forensics expert, he walked past the polished reception with practiced authority.

"We're here to review electronic files from the CEO's drive."

The receptionist paled. "Ms. Sharma isn't in right now."

"Good," Rai said. "She won't be able to interfere."

They swept through the office. The tech team began imaging every hard drive, every server node, and even the cloud access terminals. Rai found a private office, Rhea's.

Inside were whiteboards filled with logistics flowcharts, timelines, and half-erased codenames. But what caught his eye was the closed drawer under her desk. Inside it: a burner phone, wiped clean.

He bagged it.

"Sir," the tech agent said, "We found remote deletion logs on the company server. Someone initiated a wipe at 4:02 AM."

Rai smirked. "She's clever."

"Too clever?" the constable asked.

"Maybe. But no one covers their tracks perfectly."

That evening, Rhea and Kanika met on the rooftop of Kanika's flat.

"You need to create distance," Kanika said. "The media's circling. Tara's been seen at the station twice."

"She'll crack," Rhea said coldly.

"You're not worried?"

"I'm calculating."

Kanika handed her a new phone. "Pre-loaded with a secure VPN and number. Only one contact—me."

"Where's the original phone?" Rhea asked.

Kanika nodded toward a flowerpot. "Sealed and buried. Right under your daisies."

Rhea laughed. "Beautiful irony."

Kanika stared at her. "Do you ever regret it?"

Rhea's smile faded. "Regret what?"

"The deal. The clients. Arjun."

Rhea looked away. "He was stupid. But I did love him. I just loved survival more."

Tara sat across from Inspector Rai once again, the shadows under her eyes darker, her resolve harder.

"She never came home last night," Tara said. "Not once."

Rai nodded. "She doesn't need to. We're watching her."

"Is she going to be arrested?"

"Not yet. But soon."

Tara fidgeted. "If she didn't kill him, why is she hiding so much?"

"Because in Delhi," Rai said, "even the innocent can't afford to be clean."

Just then, an officer entered with a folder.

"We got partial recovery from her wiped drive. Including a document with weapons specs and overseas addresses."

Tara's breath caught.

"So it's true," she whispered.

"Yes," Rai said, looking at her carefully. "But that doesn't make her a killer. Just someone with a lot to lose."

Tara's eyes burned. "Then who did it?"

Rai didn't answer. Not yet.

Sameera Mehta stirred her tea with eerie calm as she watched the news play out on her TV.

Arjun's murder. His company's secrets. Rhea's scandal. Dhanush's silence.

Everything was going as she had hoped.

She sipped her tea.

The empire was shaking.

And no one suspected her.

Yet.

IV
What the Phone Holds

The night was silent in Greater Kailash, save for the rustle of dry leaves skimming the pavement. Beneath Rhea's balcony, a figure in a hooded jacket crouched over the flowerbed. The soil was soft, and the plastic-wrapped object was exactly where Kanika had said it would be.

With gloved hands, the figure lifted the burner phone from its temporary grave.

It wasn't Kanika.

The screen blinked to life. Password protected. But this wasn't a theft—it was a recovery.

In another corner of the city, Inspector Rai was waiting.

The phone was delivered to a forensics lab by dawn. The

data team jumped into action. The encryption was hard, but not impossible. Rai watched the screen as it flickered—one message, one image, one audio file at a time.

Arjun's voice emerged first.

"If something happens to me, look at the last folder. Backup_RheaQ4. Don't trust Rhea. And don't tell my family. Especially not Sameera."

Rai's brows shot up. "Sameera?"

A list of files followed—PDFs, bank transfers, encrypted contracts. Names in foreign scripts. Shipment tracking logs.

But the most damning was a voice memo, timestamped two days before the murder.

"Rhea, this has to stop. You're in too deep. These aren't fake exports anymore. I'm deleting the backups."

A pause.

"Unless you tell Tara. I'll give you 24 hours."

Back at her flat, Tara stood in the kitchen, staring at a coffee she hadn't touched. Her mind kept circling Arjun's last note. Not to trust Rhea. Not to trust anyone.

Her phone buzzed.

Unknown Number.

She picked up.

"I found the phone," Rai said.

Tara's breath hitched. "What's in it?"

"A lot. But more questions too. Including one about your aunt."

Tara was silent.

"I need you to stay close," he continued. "Things are moving fast."

She nodded, forgetting he couldn't see her.

Kanika paced in her studio apartment, cursing under her breath. Someone had dug up the phone. Which meant Rhea had lied. Again.

When she called her, Rhea didn't answer.

So Kanika sent a text: They have the phone. We're done.

Five minutes later, her doorbell rang.

Kanika opened it to find Rhea, soaked in rain, calm as ever.

"We need to talk," Rhea said.

Kanika stepped aside.

The door shut.

And only one of them would walk out alive.

V

The Woman Behind the Curtain

Sameera Mehta was nothing like the rest of the Mehta clan.

Where the men flaunted their power, she hoarded it like an old relic. She knew how to blend into the background, an art she had perfected over decades of charity galas, funeral speeches, and polite society.

No one noticed the woman who never raised her voice.

But Sameera noticed everything.

That morning, she sat in her sunroom, flipping through an old leather-bound journal. It was Arjun's. She'd taken it from his room the day after his death. One page in particular made her jaw tense.

"I think she knows. But she won't say it. Not until she gets what she wants."

He was talking about her.

The truth was, Arjun had always been a risk. Too honest. Too loving. Too... loyal.

And loyalty didn't serve the Mehta legacy. Not when 1500 crore was on the line.

Her son, Dhanush, had no idea what she'd done for him. The blood she had spilled to secure his future. He still thought it was some terrible mistake, that justice had misfired.

Foolish boy.

Sameera sipped her tea as the news showed Rhea's face on the screen, connected to an illegal arms network.

She smiled softly.

Let the girls destroy each other.

At the police station, Rai was piecing together what little he could from the data recovered. The phone painted a damning picture of Rhea, yes. But Arjun's note about Sameera shifted the wind.

He called Tara in.

"I need to ask you something," he said.

"Did Arjun ever tell you about his will?"

Tara shook her head. "Only that he hadn't updated it in years."

"He was going to rewrite it," Rai said. "Remove Sameera's name entirely."

Tara frowned. "But why?"

"Because he knew she was planning something. He just didn't live long enough to stop it."

Dhanush Mehta sat in his prison cell, staring at the TV bolted to the wall. The news ticker scrolled his name: Cousin of slain Arjun Mehta—still in custody pending review.

Ten years. Ten years for a crime he hadn't committed.

He ran a hand through his hair and closed his eyes. He saw Arjun smiling. Then collapsing.

Then his mother's cold hand on his shoulder the next day.

"You'll be fine," she had said.

Now, he wasn't sure what she meant.

VI

Missing Pieces, Shattered Trust

The sun had barely risen over Delhi, and Tara hadn't slept. Shadows danced on the wall from the ceiling fan spinning above, as her eyes fixated on the dusty shoebox in front of her. She'd found it tucked away at the bottom of Kanika's wardrobe while retrieving a scarf she had lent her months ago. Inside was a bundle of postcards, old birthday cards, and a flash drive.

Her hands trembled as she inserted it into her laptop.

At first, nothing.

Then a single folder appeared: TRUTH_IS_DIRTY

Tara clicked.

Her heart thudded.

Emails. Photos. Surveillance footage. Screenshots of bank transfers. And then video clips. One labeled: ARJUN_OFFICE_NIGHT_931.MP4

She opened it, chest tightening.

The timestamp showed 10:42 PM. Just ninety minutes before he was found dead.

There he was, Arjun Mehta, pacing outside Rhea's office building, talking on his phone, agitated. Rhea appears in the next frame. She's arguing. Gesturing. She grabs his arm. He shakes her off. Then she leaves the frame.

Tara slammed the laptop shut.

Her sister had lied to her.

Again.

Inspector Rai watched the footage stone-faced.

"This is new," he said.

Tara nodded. "She told me she was in Noida."

"Why would she lie unless she had something to hide?"

Rai pulled out his notebook. "We need to verify that video. And we need to find out what else Kanika was hiding."

Tara's voice cracked. "Do you think Rhea—?"

"She's involved. But I don't think she's the one who delivered the final blow."

Tara closed her eyes. It didn't make her feel better.

Across town, Rhea sat at her office desk, staring at the same footage.

Her laptop beeped. An email from an encrypted ID: They know. Bury what's left.

Rhea replied with a single word: When?

The response came seconds later: Tonight. Burn everything.

She deleted the thread.

Kanika's flash drive hadn't been the only one.

And Rhea still had the second phone, hidden in a hollow compartment in her bookshelf.

She reached for it, unlocked it with her fingerprint, and listened to the only file Arjun had saved under DO NOT DELETE.

His voice cracked.

"Rhea, you're playing a dangerous game. I told you, I'm going to Tara. I'll confess everything. About us. About the deals. About the money."

Silence.

Then:

"If you're listening to this... something went wrong."

Later that night, Tara and Rhea crossed paths in their flat's narrow hallway.

Tara's gaze was venomous.

Rhea stopped. "You've been digging."

"You lied. You were with him that night."

"So?"

"So what happened?" Tara asked. Her voice cracked with fury. "You fought with him. Did you hurt him? Did Kanika see something? Is that why she's—"

"Gone?" Rhea's voice was ice. "Be careful, Tara. Obsession makes you reckless."

Tara stepped closer. "I'm not the one hiding phones and deleting footage."

"No," Rhea whispered. "You're the one destroying yourself."

In her home, Sameera Mehta took her time stirring her tea.

She smiled faintly as she read a report: Search Warrant Filed: Mehta Estate Pending Review.

She reached into her drawer, pulled out a velvet-lined box, and inside it, a key.

To a basement.

To everything that needed to stay buried.

VII
Voicemails and Vengeance

The audio file echoed through the interrogation room like a ghost refusing to rest.

"If you're listening to this... something went wrong."

Inspector Rai hit pause.

Tara stared at the phone screen, pale and silent.

Rai looked up. "There's more."

He played the next clip.

"Rhea, this has to stop. These aren't fake shipments anymore. They're real weapons. Real clients. If you won't walk away, I'll go to the cops."

Pause. Shuffle of movement. Then—

"Don't touch me! I said, don't—"

The recording ended in static.

Rai turned the screen off. "That was 9:11 PM. We found his body at 10:52."

Tara swallowed hard. "So she was the last person to see him alive."

"She's not talking. But I've got surveillance confirming she returned to her flat at 11:10 PM. Covered in rain. And possibly blood."

Meanwhile, Rhea met with a fixer named Malik.

An underground parking garage. Midnight.

"I want all the backups gone," she said.

Malik raised an eyebrow. "You said this was about files. Not murder."

She handed him an envelope.

"It's about legacy."

He nodded. "One more job. Then we're square."

He took the envelope and vanished into the night.

The next morning, Delhi woke to a front-page headline:

"Arjun Mehta's Secret Affair Revealed: Voices from the Grave"

Attached was a leaked voicemail clip. One of Arjun's confessions to Tara about Rhea.

"I didn't mean to. It just happened. I think she's dangerous, Tara. I think... I think she's using me."

Rhea tossed the paper into her fireplace.

Then she called the number she hadn't dialed in years.

Sameera answered.

"Things are unraveling," Rhea said.

Sameera was quiet. "Let them."

"I need your help."

"You never listened. Why should I now?"

"Because if I fall, you go with me."

Sameera paused.

"Meet me. Midnight. The basement."

Rai reviewed the call logs from the night Arjun died.

One call stood out. A number registered under Dhanush's name.

But Dhanush was already in jail.

And the call had been made from the Mehta estate.

Sameera's estate.

Rai's blood ran cold.

He picked up the phone and dialed the judge.

"Unseal the basement. Now."

Tara received a USB drive by courier. No return address.

Inside: one video file. Kanika. Tear-streaked, sitting in front of her laptop.

"If you're watching this, something happened to me. Rhea... she's dangerous. But she's not the only one. Look into the will. Look at Sameera. And for god's sake—protect Dhanush. He doesn't know."

Tara's knees buckled.

Arjun. Kanika. Dhanush.

One by one, everyone she loved was either dead, silenced, or framed.

Now it was her turn to decide.

Run.

Or fight.

VIII
Inheritance Clause 32B

The morning light hit the side of Tara's face as she walked into the lawyer's office, her hands clutching the letter Arjun had written but never sent. The handwriting was unmistakable, curved in his usual rushed scrawl. Inside, he detailed changes he intended to make to his will, removing Sameera and replacing her stake with a non-profit that funded mental health rehabilitation.

Arjun had written, "If anything happens to me, Clause 32B is the key. It's not just about money. It's about what they did with it."

The lawyer, a sharp woman named Farzana who had worked with the Mehtas for years, flipped through the draft silently. Her hands paused on the final clause.

"If this had been filed," she whispered, "Sameera would've

been completely cut out. And Dhanush would've become the controlling heir."

Tara blinked. "So she had motive."

"More than you know," Farzana said, handing her an old file labeled "Mehta Estate – Pending Amendments."

Within it, handwritten notes from Arjun. Audit trails. Cryptic warnings. A diagram of how money from the estate was being funneled through shell companies, some linked back to a familiar name: BlackOrchid Logistics.

Tara froze. That was Rhea's company.

And the first shell company listed?

Sameera Holdings Pvt Ltd.

Rai watched from across the street as Sameera emerged from the central registrar's building. He didn't need to follow her. He already knew where she was going.

But more importantly, he knew what she had to lose.

"Send a copy of the amendment to the commissioner," he told his deputy. "And mark it urgent."

Meanwhile, in the basement of the Mehta estate, Rhea and Sameera stood face to face.

"You lied to me," Rhea hissed. "You said it would all pass. That no one would dig this deep."

"You were careless," Sameera replied. "You let emotion get in the way."

"He loved me. You didn't have to kill him."

Sameera blinked. "I didn't kill him because he loved you. I killed him because he threatened our bloodline."

"You mean your money."

Sameera stepped closer. "If I had to do it again, I would. You're my niece. But Dhanush is my son. I protect what's mine."

Rhea's hands trembled.

But she said nothing.

For now.

IX

The Interrogation Room

The interrogation room was always cold.

A strategy, Rai had said once. Keep them uncomfortable. Off balance.

Rhea sat perfectly composed, arms folded, lips untouched by color, eyes dark as obsidian. Across from her, Rai placed the evidence on the table: a burner phone, a bloodstained ledger, a flash drive.

"We found this in Kanika's storage locker," he began. "Do you know what it is?"

"No."

"It's your voice."

He hit play.

"You think I did this for you? I did it for my son."

And then Rhea's voice: "You think he'll forgive you when he finds out?"

Rhea listened without flinching. "That proves nothing."

Rai raised a brow. "So you admit that's your voice?"

"No. I'm saying it proves nothing."

Tara watched from the other side of the one-way mirror, rage blooming in her chest.

"She's not even afraid," she whispered.

"She doesn't know what fear is," Rai replied.

After the session, Rai walked Rhea out under armed escort.

Before stepping into the police vehicle, she turned to him and whispered, "You're chasing ghosts, Inspector. And ghosts don't bleed."

He didn't respond. But in his pocket, he held a new warrant.

This time, not for Rhea.

But for Sameera Mehta.

Back at the station, Tara sifted through more recovered files.

Among them, a video Arjun had labeled "FINAL INSURANCE."

He sat at his desk, pale and tired.

"If I don't come home, look into the will. Look into Rhea. But most of all, don't trust the one who says the least. The one who watches it all happen and sips her tea."

Tara's tears fell silently.

The final frame showed Arjun holding a key.

The same key Tara found inside Sameera's guestroom drawer.

The key to the Mehta estate's basement.

By midnight, the lock turned.

And what they found inside would crack the case open.

Forever.

X

The Sister Knows Nothing

The media storm was relentless. Headlines flashed across Delhi: "Sister or Suspect?" "Torn by Blood, Tied by Death." And always, photos of Tara, crying, walking, speaking, breathing, without her permission, without her context.

Rhea had finally played her trump card.

The leaked therapy files were real. A year ago, Tara had gone through a breakdown after losing her job and struggling in her relationship with Arjun. The sessions, recorded and transcribed, were never meant to be public.

But now, they were viral.

"She's emotionally unstable," Rhea's statement read. "I worry for her. I just want her to get help."

Tara stared at the news feed on her phone, frozen. Betrayal had a new face. It was wearing a mask of concern.

In the police station, Rai slammed the printout of the article onto his desk. "Who leaked this?"

His deputy shrugged. "Could've come from anywhere."

"Find out."

Tara arrived at the station with her hair tied in a bun, a folder under her arm. Her eyes burned, but her voice was steel.

"I'm done being quiet."

She dropped the folder on his desk.

Inside were Arjun's handwritten notes, cross-referencing dates, companies, and initials. At the bottom, a scribbled name: 'S Holdings'.

"Sameera?" Rai asked.

"Or Satan. Your call."

Sameera watched from her terrace as reporters camped outside her gates. Her phone rang.

"Madam, you've been summoned," said a voice.

Sameera took a deep breath, exhaled slowly, and said, "Delay it."

"You can't delay a warrant."

"I can delay anything," she replied. And hung up.

In prison, Dhanush received a letter with no return address.

Inside: a note in Arjun's handwriting.

D – If you get this, I didn't send it. That means she did. You were right. Trust no one but Tara. I love you, brother.

Dhanush pressed the note to his chest.

For the first time in ten years, he cried.

XI

Deleted, Not Forgotten

Inspector Rai's tech team had been working overtime.

The files recovered from Kanika's storage had been partially corrupted, but a young officer named Nikhil managed to salvage a handful of audio logs and two surveillance backups.

One clip showed Kanika talking to someone on the phone.

"I have everything. I'll meet you tonight at the old Metro yard."

Timestamp: 10:38 PM. The same night, Arjun was killed.

Another clip revealed something else. The angle was poor, but a figure with a limp entered a building carrying a plastic bag. The figure wore gloves and left with the bag empty.

Sameera had a limp. Old knee surgery.

Rai circled the figure on the screen. "We're getting close."

Tara stood beside him. "We're already there."

Meanwhile, Rhea was unraveling.

Her contact, Malik, had gone underground. She couldn't reach Kanika's cousin, who had agreed to hide the secondary backup. The net was closing.

And Sameera wasn't picking up her calls.

She stood in her bathroom, staring at her reflection.

"You'll be fine," she told herself. "You always are."

But her voice cracked on the last word.

She opened her safe.

Inside was a revolver.

She didn't take it out. Not yet.

Just knowing it was there calmed her.

At night, Rai's team ran a deep scan on the burner phone they'd recovered from the Mehta estate basement.

A deleted folder appeared: "Blue Orchid Clients."

Inside: Names. Accounts. Shipments. Dates.

Every transaction linked to Rhea's company.

Every payment cleared through a signature.

Sameera's.

Rai picked up his phone and called the commissioner.

"We have it. Call the judge. I want them both arrested. Now."

Back at the estate, Sameera stood in front of her old wedding portrait.

"You were right," she whispered to her late husband's image. "Love makes us weak."

Then she turned and walked to her study, where a single piece of evidence sat burning in the fireplace.

But it was too late.

Truth, like ash, rises eventually.

XII

A Perfect Love Story Ruined

Tara sat on the floor of her bedroom, a mess of torn photo albums and handwritten letters scattered around her like debris after a storm. She held the object she had avoided for weeks, Arjun's personal journal.

It was bound in soft black leather, worn at the edges. She inhaled deeply before opening it.

The first page read:

"To the one I trusted most, if you're reading this, it means I didn't get the chance to say everything out loud."

She turned page after page. Some pages were filled with mundane notes, ideas for startups, and half-written love poems. Others held pain. Doubt. And most damning, regret.

Then she found it. A loose sheet tucked into the back.

"Tara, I thought loving you would make me brave. But now I see that it made me reckless. I should have told you about Rhea. I should have told you everything."

Tears streamed down her cheeks, but she read on.

"There's something deeply wrong in my family. Sameera knows everything. She controls everything. I think... she's done things no one would believe."

The final page chilled her.

"I meet her tonight. The will is ready. Clause 32B will protect Dhanush, and I'm leaving Rhea out. I need to make things right."

The entry was dated the day he died.

At the same moment, Rai sat in his office staring at a forensic report. It confirmed a half-burned document recovered from Sameera's fireplace. The title was barely legible: "Estate Adjustment – Mehta Holdings".

There were also traces of blood on the envelope.

He picked up the phone.

"Get me a search team. We're going into the Mehta estate basement. Tonight."

That afternoon, Tara watched Rhea speak to the press. Dressed in muted tones, eyes brimming with well-practiced sorrow.

"We've all lost someone we loved," she said. "But turning on each other won't bring him back."

Tara clenched her jaw.

Not two weeks ago, that same voice leaked her therapy records to the media.

Later that evening, she stood outside Rhea's door.

"I need to see the other phone," she said flatly.

Rhea didn't even blink. "I don't have it."

"You hid it with Kanika. You knew she wouldn't betray you."

Silence.

Tara stepped forward. "She's dead because of you. So is Arjun."

That hit something.

Rhea finally looked away. "I loved him."

"So did I," Tara said. "The difference is, he loved me back."

And she walked away.

Sameera stared out the window, sipping tea like she always did at dusk.

But tonight, her fingers trembled slightly.

XIII

Midnight Witness

The knock on Inspector Rai's door came just after midnight. When he opened it, he found a man in a crumpled uniform standing awkwardly.

"Sir... I worked night duty at Rhea Sharma's office. The night Arjun died."

Inside the station, the man's name, Ramesh, was scribbled into an interview log.

He told Rai about the night.

"I saw her," he whispered. "Not Rhea. The older woman. Sameera. She walked in through the back gate. Alone. She had a plastic bag in one hand and was limping badly."

"What time?" Rai asked.

"A little after ten."

"And she left?"

"Fifteen minutes later. Without the bag."

Rai leaned back. "You ever see her before that?"

"No. But I know that limp. Everyone does."

Tara visited Dhanush in prison for the first time.

His eyes were sunken, but his smile was sincere.

"I've been watching you on TV," he said. "You look strong."

Tara chuckled dryly. "I feel broken."

"You're the only one still looking for the truth."

She passed him a note, Arjun's final words from his journal.

He read them in silence. When he looked up, his face was pale.

"He... he was going to fix everything?"

"Yes."

"And she stopped him."

Tara didn't need to say who.

Rhea came home to find a file on her kitchen table.

Inside, photos of Sameera meeting with Malik, the fixer.

And an invoice marked "Surveillance Clean-up – Completed."

On the last page: Kanika's name.

Her scream rattled the windows.

She finally understood.

Sameera had been cleaning house.

And Rhea was next.

At the Mehta estate basement, Rai and his team broke through a sealed iron door.

Inside, ledgers, hard drives, two safes, and old security tapes.

One of them was labeled "July 17th – Last Entry – Arjun."

Rai inserted the tape.

The footage played.

Arjun entered the room. Sameera followed.

They argued. The sound had no audio, but the body language was unmistakable.

Arjun turned to leave.

Sameera reached for the vase on the shelf.

The screen turned black.

XIV

Property, Blood & Greed

The Mehta estate boardroom had never been louder.

Voices clashed. Accusations flew. The air buzzed with tension as Tara stood alone at the head of the table, holding a manila folder in her hand.

"Arjun's final wish was to leave his legacy to Dhanush. He had proof of corruption. He was rewriting his will, Clause 32B is real, and this," she lifted the folder, "is everything he collected before he died."

The board fell silent as she laid out documentation: signatures, payments, accounts in Rhea's name, all tied to shell companies. At the top of the spiderweb: Sameera Mehta.

A nervous lawyer, Farzana, nodded at her.

"If these documents are verified, the estate must be frozen. Effective immediately."

"But the will wasn't filed," barked an older man.

"Because Arjun died before he could," Tara said. "Ask yourselves, why?"

Somewhere in the darkened wing of the estate, Sameera watched the live-streamed board meeting on a private tablet.

She sipped her tea.

She didn't flinch.

One by one, board members raised their hands to vote. The majority agreed to suspend Sameera's control and call in a government audit.

The Mehta empire, the symbol of generations, was starting to rot from within.

And Tara had lit the first match.

Inspector Rai paced his office, staring at the large printout of the Mehta family financial tree. It all connected: Sameera's shell companies, BlackOrchid's dummy accounts, offshore holdings in Cyprus.

But what made his skin crawl was a ₹8 crore payment made the night before Arjun's murder.

No name. No invoice. Just a timestamp.

He picked up his phone.

"Freeze every account linked to Sameera Mehta. I don't care who tries to stop it."

That night, Rhea sat in her apartment, lights off, the echo of her sister's text replaying in her mind.

"They know."

Attached was a still image: Sameera dragging a bag through the basement corridor.

For a moment, Rhea forgot how to breathe.

She had loved Arjun.

She had feared Sameera.

And now, both were ghosts that haunted her.

She opened the drawer.

The revolver still sat inside.

Tara returned home late. As she stepped out of her car, a blast rocked the air.

The vehicle behind her burst into flames, glass, fire, and smoke.

Had she been a few seconds slower, she wouldn't be alive.

Her phone buzzed with a blocked number.

A text.

"Next time, you won't be so lucky."

XV

The Hidden Best Friend

Delhi was reeling.

News channels spun wild theories. Was it a political conspiracy? A business hit? A lover's revenge?

Only a handful of people knew the truth.

And one of them had been pulled from the Yamuna that morning.

Kanika Sharma.

The autopsy confirmed what Rai had suspected. She'd been dead for over a week. Wrist fractures. Bruised ribs. Cause of death: blunt force trauma to the head. Her body had been wrapped in a bedsheet, weighted, and tossed.

But in her coat pocket, her phone had survived.

And inside that phone was everything.

In a locked evidence room, Rai and his cyber team uncovered folders labeled:
- KANIKA_LAST_RECORDINGS
- RHEA_CONFESSION
- SAMEERA_INSTRUCTIONS
He pressed play on the first audio file.
Rhea's voice: slurred, emotional, scared.
"I didn't want him to die. I just wanted him to stop. She said it wouldn't go that far... Kanika, I think she planned it all along."
Another clip.
Kanika's voice: "If you're hearing this, something's happened. Rhea's scared. I'm scared. Sameera is controlling everything. She had Arjun followed. And now she's watching me too."
Tara stood at the morgue, staring at the body behind the glass.
Kanika's face, once full of warmth, was bruised and pale.

A tear ran down Tara's cheek.

"You died protecting the truth," she whispered. "I won't let it be in vain."

That night, Rhea was picked up by plainclothes officers.

She didn't scream. Didn't run.

At the station, Rai placed a file in front of her.

"You're not being charged with murder. Not yet."

"What then?"

"Conspiracy. Suppression of evidence. Aiding in obstruction. Want to go for an accessory after the fact while we're at it?"

Rhea chuckled. "So poetic."

"No," he said, coldly. "That was your sister."

Sameera didn't answer when Rhea called from jail.
Didn't return the messages.
Didn't speak in her defense.
Rhea sat on her cot in silence.
She had been many things: sharp, ambitious, cold.
But never naive.
Until now.
She had finally understood.
Sameera didn't protect her family. She protected power.

XVI

Phones That Shouldn't Ring

Tara was jolted awake by the sound of her phone vibrating violently on her bedside table.

It was 3:02 AM.

The screen read: Private Number.

She hesitated.

Then answered.

Static. Then a voice.

"Tara. Don't go to the press. They're listening."

The call cut out.

She stared at the phone. The number wasn't traceable.

She called Rai.

"We need to talk. Now."

Inspector Rai met her at a quiet tea stall just off Connaught Place. No uniforms. No files. Just him, her, and two cups of chai.

"There's a leak," Tara said. "Whoever killed Arjun is watching every move we make."

Rai nodded. "I've suspected it for weeks. I kept things off the record."

He took out a second phone, a clean burner, and slid it to her.

"Use this. If they're watching you, they'll intercept anything digital."

Back at the estate, Sameera sat at her vanity table, brushing her hair with slow, deliberate strokes.

Her phone buzzed.

A message from an encrypted ID: "She's digging again. You need to end this."

She turned off the phone.

She wasn't going to run.

Not yet.

At the police lab, Nikhil, the junior tech who had cracked Kanika's drive, found something in the metadata of the surveillance tapes.

A pattern.

Every footage file that involved Sameera had been edited. Not deleted—backdated.

The timecodes were all altered.

He rushed to tell Rai.

"You were right. She didn't just hide. She rewrote the timeline."

Rai grinned darkly. "That's a mistake. Because now, we know exactly where to look."

That night, Tara received a second call.

Same eerie static. Then a different voice.

"She's been in the system for decades. If you want to survive, burn everything and walk away."

The call ended.

Tara didn't sleep that night.

But she didn't burn anything.

She made copies.

XVII
Backdated Emails

The next morning, a courier arrived at the police station with no return label.

Inside the package: a stack of printed emails. Dozens of them.

All backdated. All seemingly between Arjun and a contact named "S Holdings."

Rai scanned the headers. The servers didn't match. They were sent through rerouted domains.

Fake.

But someone wanted them to look real.

A digital forensic sweep revealed something chilling: the emails had been planted the night before Kanika died.

Tara sat at her dining table, folders spread across the table like an autopsy. She'd highlighted timelines, cross-checked call logs, and matched GPS data.

There was one inconsistency she couldn't explain.

Sameera's driver, Deepak, had logged a vehicle maintenance report during the night of the murder. But the odometer showed a 120 km discrepancy.

She drove somewhere that night.

And it wasn't on record.

Tara took a deep breath.

It was time to confront the last person who might still talk.

Sameera's former housekeeper, Meera, lived in a two-room tenement in South Delhi. Tara arrived unannounced, holding a photo of Arjun.

Meera's eyes welled up.

"He used to visit us during Diwali," she said. "Always remembered my son's name."

Tara placed her hand on hers. "I need the truth. Anything."

Meera nodded slowly.

"That night, madam left with gloves on. Said she was going to end something."

Meanwhile, Rai received a final report from the cyber team.

They'd traced a signal from a now-defunct relay tower used only by military contractors.

It pinged twice.

Once at the Mehta estate.

Once outside Kanika's apartment.

The killer had used government-grade tech.

Someone powerful was covering their tracks.

But the trail was no longer cold.

It was burning.

XVIII

The Whistleblower Files

Tara waited at the edge of Nehru Park, her fingers nervously tracing the edge of a small brown envelope. A stranger had contacted her, a former employee of BlackOrchid Logistics. He said he had something that could crack the entire case.

At 7:04 PM, a young man in a windbreaker and glasses approached her, face shadowed by a cap.

"Name's Aseem," he said. "I used to run backend logistics at Rhea's company. Until she made me change shipment codes."

Tara handed him a second phone. "Talk."

Aseem revealed what he knew: doctored invoices, blacklisted weapons tagged as 'spare parts,' and most shocking, an encrypted USB drive Kanika had given him.

"She said if anything happened to her, give it to someone who could finish what Arjun started."

Inspector Rai stared at the decrypted contents later that night.

It was all there.

Names of officials, dates, bribes, weapon types, shipment ports, and an entire ecosystem of black-market transactions.

And at the top of the flowchart: S Holdings, aka Sameera Mehta.

Farzana, the lawyer, returned from Cyprus with documents from one of the estate's dormant offshore accounts. One of the listed owners?

Dhanush Mehta.

But he had never signed any of the paperwork.

Farzana confirmed the signatures were forged. And the date? Two days after Arjun's death.

Rai stared at the scan.

Sameera had planned it all down to the second.

Back in jail, Rhea watched the evening news.

A special investigative piece now showed her company's involvement with gun smuggling.

She didn't deny it.

But in the corner of her cell, she wrote something on a piece of toilet paper and folded it like origami.

"If I go down, I take her with me."

Tara walked into the station that evening, holding Aseem's drive.

She met Rai's eyes.

"We have our whistleblower."

And it was time to blow everything open.

XIX

Operation BlackOrchid

Operation BlackOrchid launched at 4:00 AM.

Code-named by Rai himself, the mission involved two dozen officers, three cyber-forensic vans, and a set of coordinated raids across Delhi, Mumbai, and Hyderabad.

Every shell company, warehouse, and data center tied to the Mehta estate was hit simultaneously.

At 4:22 AM, officers entered the private archives of BlackOrchid's Noida office.

Inside: hundreds of paper files, flash drives, and backup disks.

Evidence of twenty years of smuggling.

And then, at 4:37 AM, something unexpected.

A photo.

Arjun, smiling beside Sameera, holding a document labeled "Partnership Agreement – S Holdings & BlackOrchid".

Signed six months before his death.

Rai studied the photo, frowning.

"Why would he sign that?" he asked.

Tara said softly, "Unless he didn't know what it really was."

By dawn, the headlines roared:

"MEHTA FAMILY UNDER FIRE – RACKET SPANS THREE STATES"

"BLACKORCHID SCANDAL EXPLODES – GUN DEALS TIED TO POLITICAL FIGURES"

A press conference was scheduled.

Rai would finally speak.

Sameera remained silent in her mansion.

But the warrants had arrived.

And so had the press vans.

She turned on her television.

Rhea was giving a jailhouse interview.

"She told me it was just money transfers. That no one would get hurt. I was wrong."

Sameera didn't blink.

She simply picked up the phone.

"Activate the contingency."

The voice on the other end replied, "Understood."

At that exact moment, Tara's second phone began ringing.

Unknown number.

She answered.

"She's planning to disappear. You have less than 48 hours."

Then the call ended.

No trace.

No echo.

But Tara knew it was real.

They had uncovered the truth.

Now they had to survive it.

XX

A Deal with the Devil

Sameera Mehta stood at the tall windows of her private study, staring out at the front lawns of her estate. Beyond the trimmed hedges and high iron gates, the world was beginning to turn against her.

She knew this feeling. It wasn't fear. It was anticipation.

She had survived worse.

A phone call. A war. A death.

What was one more crisis?

She walked slowly to the mahogany bar, poured herself a drink, and dialed the one number she swore she'd never call again.

The Chief Minister answered on the second ring.

"You've got nerve," he said.

"I have leverage," she replied. "And right now, you need me alive more than I need freedom."

"I can't protect you from this."

"You can slow it down."

Silence.

Then, reluctantly: "You have seventy-two hours. Then I walk away."

Sameera smiled faintly. "That's all I need."

Across Delhi, Operation BlackOrchid was front-page news.

Reporters swarmed outside police stations. TV anchors speculated about smuggled weapons and corrupt deals.

Inspector Rai held a press conference flanked by officers and cybercrime analysts.

"We are investigating a multi-level criminal enterprise that involves financial fraud, black-market arms, and obstruction of justice," Rai said firmly. "This is not just about the Mehta family. This is about the nation."

Tara watched from the back of the room, standing in the shadows.

Her phone buzzed. An unknown number.

A voice whispered:

"She's planning her exit. She has a jet waiting in Jaipur. Midnight, Saturday."

She hung up.

She didn't need to ask who "she" was.

Sameera was running.

Unless they stopped her.

Later that night, Sameera opened a safe built into the floor of her bedroom. Inside were stacks of cash, two passports, a gun, and a small velvet pouch.

She took the pouch and sat at her vanity table.

Inside was a single cufflink.

Arjun's.

Bloodstained.

She stared at it for a long time before closing the pouch again.

Not regret.

Just a remembrance.

XXI

Dhanush Speaks

For ten years, Dhanush Mehta had lived in the shadow of a lie.

He had eaten in silence. Prayed in silence. Suffered in silence.

But when Rai visited his prison cell and slid a manila envelope across the table, containing Arjun's real will, the forged documents, and Kanika's voice memos, something inside him shifted.

"I'll testify," he said.

Rai nodded slowly. "It will be dangerous."

"I don't care anymore. I won't let her rewrite my story."

A day later, the prison gates opened for Dhanush under high-security escort.

He wasn't free, not yet. But he was protected.

At a safe house outside Delhi, he met Tara for the first time in years.

She stood at the doorway, arms stiff at her sides, unsure of what to say.

He hugged her first.

"I'm sorry," she said into his shoulder.

"You fought," he replied. "That's enough."

They sat together, reviewing every file, email, and testimony they now had.

It was overwhelming.

But for the first time, they weren't alone.

Later that night, Dhanush recorded a public statement from the safe house.

His voice was steady, his eyes clear.

"My name is Dhanush Mehta. I was framed for a crime I didn't commit. My cousin, Arjun, was murdered to protect a lie. And that lie ends today."

Rai stood behind the camera, nodding once.

In the Mehta mansion, Sameera watched the broadcast without blinking.

When it ended, she turned off the screen.

And for the first time in years, she didn't reach for her tea.

She reached for her gun.

XXII

One Last Flight

The private jet sat gleaming on the tarmac at Jaipur International Airport. No logos. No tail number. Inside, the pilot reviewed coordinates for a non-disclosed location on the Swiss border.

At precisely 11:32 PM, Sameera Mehta stepped out of a black SUV, flanked by two silent men in charcoal suits. She wore no jewelry, no lipstick, and no emotion. Just a tailored coat, leather gloves, and an envelope of final instructions.

Inside the hangar, a satellite phone buzzed on the console.

"Landing clear. Window: 28 minutes. Then airspace closes."

Sameera nodded once. She handed her assistant a flash drive.

"If anything happens to me," she said, "deliver this to the Minister of Defence."

He looked startled.

"I mean it."

He hesitated, then took it and disappeared down the runway.

Back in Delhi, Tara sat in the passenger seat of Rai's jeep, the city flashing past in streaks of orange light.

"She's really going to do it," Tara muttered. "She's going to vanish."

"Not if we stop her," Rai said, jaw tight. "Intercept call logs came in from Jaipur Air Command. She's booked to lift off any minute."

Tara gripped her seatbelt.

"How long do we have?"

"Thirty minutes. Less if she skips protocol."

Dhanush sat in the safehouse, watching a news segment on the raid.

His phone buzzed.

A private number.

He answered.

Sameera's voice was soft.

"You were always my weakness."

He stood up, silent.

"I did it all for you."

"No," he whispered. "You did it for yourself."

She paused. "Goodbye, beta."

And then the call ended.

Dhanush threw the phone against the wall.

At Jaipur runway security, a white unmarked van pulled up.

Rai leapt out first.

"Delhi Police. We have jurisdiction. Seal the runway now."

The ground staff hesitated.

Then sirens pierced the air.

Sameera looked up from her seat as the jet's door hissed open.

A flood of red and blue lights illuminated the hangar.

She didn't run.

She didn't fight.

She simply pulled off her gloves, folded them in her lap, and waited.

As Rai stepped into the cabin, she smiled.

"Took you long enough."

XXIII

Redemption Isn't Cheap

The courtroom was packed. Not with the public, this trial was sealed. But journalists still found ways to get quotes, leak recordings, and fuel headlines.

"Matriarch of Murder," they called her.

"India's Shadow Queen."

Sameera sat at the defense table, elegant as ever. Her hair was neatly tied back. Her suit pressed. Her silence was complete.

Across the aisle, Dhanush sat beside Tara, his hands clenched.

The judge read the charges: murder, conspiracy, financial fraud, obstruction of justice, arms trafficking.

Rhea was brought in briefly as a key witness. She looked pale, stripped of defiance.

She met Tara's eyes for only a second.

Then lowered her gaze.

In his testimony, Dhanush told the court about Arjun's last days, Sameera's conversations, and the night he was arrested.

"She told me to stay quiet. That it would all blow over. That they needed someone to blame."

He paused.

"I was that someone."

His voice didn't waver.

Tara followed with the digital trail, voice memos, GPS logs, and Kanika's final recordings.

Even the defense stopped objecting.

There was no point.

After nine days of trial, the verdict was delivered.

Guilty on all counts.

Sameera blinked once.

Then nodded.

As she was led away in cuffs, she passed Dhanush.

He didn't flinch.

But for a brief moment, he saw her as she once was: powerful, poised, and untouchable.

And now?

Just another ghost in the system.

That evening, Tara stood alone at Arjun's favorite spot by the riverbank. The water shimmered under the city lights.

She dropped a rose into the current.

"For you," she whispered. "For everything you tried to protect."

Behind her, Dhanush approached slowly.

"Ready?" he asked.

She smiled.

"Now we write the real story."

XXIV

The Book That Reopened the Case

Ten years later.

The city had changed, but its memory hadn't.

A crisp autumn morning rolled through Delhi's streets as a new face entered the national library—one with a long notebook, a tape recorder, and a very specific name on his checklist.

Dilip Bose, investigative journalist turned best-selling true-crime author.

His last book exposed a minister's scandal in West Bengal.

This one, however, was personal.

"Phones, Lies & Bloodlines: The Mehta Chronicles" was

going to be his masterpiece.

But as he sifted through old case files, whispers resurfaced.

Some transcripts didn't match the official verdict.

Some testimonies were missing entire pages.

And the name "Kanika" appeared in records long after her confirmed death.

He called Tara first.

She answered, cautious but firm.

"I'm not doing interviews."

"I don't want your quotes," Dilip said. "I want your insight. The timeline... it's off."

Pause.

Then: "Meet me at Arjun's memorial. Tonight. No press."

The memorial stood in silence under a canopy of rustling trees.

Dilip arrived early, clutching a slim file.

Tara showed up fifteen minutes later.

He handed her a photograph.

"Taken two months after the case was closed."

Tara stared.

It was a grainy CCTV image. A woman in sunglasses. Dark coat.

The file read: Subject ID: K Sharma. Status: Unknown.

"But Kanika's dead," Tara whispered.

"Or someone wanted you to believe she was."

Dilip leaned closer.

"There's one more recording. Buried in the court archives. Labeled 'unauthenticated.'"

Tara's heartbeat quickened.

"What's on it?"

Dilip stared at the sky.

"A voice. Familiar. But not who you'd expect."

XXV

The Final Recordings

The file was stored deep in the legal vault under the Delhi High Court.

Accessing it took weeks, layers of red tape, authorization requests, and a paper trail Dilip was careful to manipulate.

When he finally slipped the drive into his laptop, the room was silent.

He hit play.

The recording crackled. Then a voice emerged.

Soft. Shaky.

"This is Kanika Sharma. If I'm dead, it's because I chose to run. I know what you think, but the truth is... Sameera wasn't working alone."

Dilip's eyes narrowed.

"Rhea?"

"No," the voice continued. "She was protecting someone else. Someone none of you ever suspected."

A long pause.

"Arjun had a secret. One he took to the grave. But it didn't die with him."

Click.

End of file.

Dilip called Tara immediately.

"You need to hear this."

They met again. This time at the edge of Yamuna.

He played the file.

Tara went pale.

"I remember that night," she whispered. "He said something... just before he left. That he had something to confess."

She looked up at Dilip.

"What if Arjun wasn't the only one being hunted?"

That evening, Dilip dug deeper.

Archived emails from Arjun's personal account.

One labeled "Re: Backups – For safety, not leverage."

Inside: a list of six names. Five were familiar.

The sixth?

A judge from Arjun's case.

Still serving.

Dilip sat back.

There were still threads.

Still shadows.

And the case that ended ten years ago?

Wasn't over.

Not really.

XXVI

The Unnamed Witness

Dilip Bose had never seen a classified vault before. He'd broken stories involving warlords and wire fraud, but this was the first time he needed a court insider to sneak him into a judiciary records annex in the dead of night.

The hall was cold. Clean. Lit by the hum of fluorescent tubes. Room 304 housed sealed cases—ones not destroyed, just buried.

He found the file by the edge of the shelf, stamped in red: WITNESS C-11 – PROTECTION ORDER INDEFINITE.

Inside were just two pages.

The transcript of a voice. No name. No video. Just a recording and a court stenographer's line-by-line entry.

"I told Arjun Mehta not to pursue it. He wouldn't listen. He thought exposing Sameera would stop it. But it wasn't just her. They were all in on it."

"Who?"

"The ones who funded the trial. The ones who hid the surveillance blueprints. You want a name? Look in the telecom security committee. Project Vahana."

Dilip blinked. His throat went dry.

He'd heard of Project Vahana once—buried in a decade-old military budget draft. Rumored to be an ultra-clandestine surveillance web involving biometric tracking and predictive behavioral data.

And Arjun had found it?

He shoved the file into his bag and left without looking back.

That night, he met Tara in a parked car off Lodhi Road.

He handed her the transcript.

She read it once, then again, slower.

"Project Vahana," she repeated, stunned. "Arjun never said anything."

"Maybe he didn't want to put you in danger."

Tara leaned back in the seat. "He always told me... if he ever disappeared, it wouldn't be because of love. It'd be because of something bigger than he could fight."

She stared out the windshield. "This is bigger."

The next morning, Tara received a text.

UNKNOWN NUMBER: "Stop digging. He died for a reason."

Attached was a live image.

Her.

Taken from across the street just two minutes ago.

She dropped the phone.

Dilip looked at her.

"We're in it now, aren't we?"

She nodded, heart pounding.

"Oh yes. And they're watching everything."

XXVII

Dead Men's Inbox

The hard drive was buried deep in the layers of encrypted folders Kanika had hidden in her safety locker. Dilip cracked the last layer using a decryption key passed to them by the whistleblower, Aseem.

Inside were 189 emails.

All from Arjun.

None of them had ever been sent.

Tara hovered over his inbox, heart in her throat. The subject lines were brutal in their simplicity:

"If I don't make it tomorrow..."

"To Dhanush: I tried."

"Tara must never know about A."

She clicked on the one labeled "A".

"You said we'd be safe once I handed over the drive. I kept my end. You didn't keep yours. You think burying Project Vahana makes us untouchable? It doesn't. I'm leaking it. And I'm telling Tara everything."

The timestamp: 12 hours before he was killed.

There was no reply.

No sender address.

Just a digital signature: :RA:

Dilip's breath caught in his throat.

"That's a digital key. From law enforcement. High-level. Possibly CBI."

Tara leaned forward. "Wait... :RA:... could that be—?"

She didn't finish the sentence.

Because the only person they knew with those initials, operating this close to the case...

Was Rai.

Inspector Dhritirashtra Rai.

Dilip closed the laptop.

"We need to be sure."

Tara shook her head, hollow.

"If he helped cover this... if he let Arjun die..."

The room was still.

Then her phone buzzed again.

One email. Sent from Arjun's hidden account.

Subject: "Safety, not leverage."

The email body had just one line:

"Meet me where we first said goodbye."

Attached was a GPS pin.

Tara's mouth dropped open.

"That's not possible."

Dilip stared.

"What?"

"That place? That's the café where Arjun broke up with me."

She swallowed hard.

"But it was torn down seven years ago."

XXVIII
A Familiar Stranger

The old café had been reduced to nothing but rubble, overtaken by weeds and half-built scaffolding. All that remained was a rusted iron gate and part of a faded sign that once read "Chai Break".

Tara stood at the GPS-marked spot.

"This makes no sense," she said, scanning the ruins.

Dilip checked the coordinates again. "We're exactly where the email pointed."

Just then, a flicker of movement caught Tara's eye near the far side of the rubble. A man stood in the shadow of an abandoned cement mixer. Not approaching. Just watching.

She took a step forward.

"Hello?"

He didn't flinch.

Dilip moved protectively in front of her, hand in his coat pocket.

The man finally walked forward—slowly, cautiously.

Tara's breath caught in her throat.

He looked like Kanika. Same jawline. Same eyes.

"Who are you?" she asked.

The man paused, then said:

"My name is Krish Sharma. Kanika's brother."

Tara staggered back. "That's not possible. She said she had no family."

"She said that to protect us."

Dilip jumped in. "Where is she? We need her to—"

Krish cut him off.

"She's alive. But only just. She's in hiding. And she sent me."

Tara's heart raced. "Why?"

Krish looked between them, cautious.

"Because she thinks one of you is working with them."

Later, at a discreet motel on the edge of the city, Krish laid out what he knew.

"Kanika ran after she found out Arjun wasn't just targeted by Sameera. There was someone else. Someone who gave Sameera his location that night."

Dilip narrowed his eyes. "Rhea?"

Krish shook his head. "No. She was caught in the middle. The real betrayal came from inside Arjun's circle."

Tara swallowed. "Who?"

Krish's silence was answer enough.

"She's not sure yet. But she said if you found the backup logs and the tracker logs, it would lead you to the person who tipped Sameera off."

"And where are those?" Tara asked.

Krish stared at her, then reached into his coat.

He handed her a flash drive.

"She said to give you this. But be careful. The last time someone tried to open it... they died."

XXIX

The Yamuna Tape

The flash drive's contents were heavily encrypted. It took Aseem nearly six hours to crack the partition.

Inside was a single folder labeled: "Yamuna_Tape_001"

Tara clicked it open.

A grainy video loaded. The timestamp was dated two nights before Arjun's murder.

The footage began with Arjun seated on a bench near the Yamuna riverbank. Beside him sat Kanika, hood pulled over her head.

The wind whipped through the audio, but their voices were clear.

Kanika: "Don't release it yet. It's not safe."

Arjun: "They need to know. People are dying, Kanika. And I think... I think it goes even further."

Kanika: "You don't understand. The judge... he's not just complicit. He's connected."

Arjun: "To what?"

Kanika: "...To your father."

The video flickered.

Kanika: "Arjun... Sameera isn't your aunt."

Arjun froze.

Arjun: "What are you saying?"

Kanika: "She's your mother."

Silence.

Kanika: "And your father... was Justice Rajnath Awasthi."

Tara's mouth dropped open.

She whispered, "The same judge who presided over his inheritance?"

Dilip looked equally stunned.

Kanika's voice returned:

Kanika: "They killed him. Years ago. Said it was a heart attack. But it wasn't. It was to ensure Sameera inherited his political ties. She's been running The Circle ever since."

The video ended abruptly.

Tara sat back, shaken.

"So he was born into it."

Dilip nodded slowly.

"He never stood a chance."

XXX
Family Tree Rewritten

The DNA file sat on the table like a bomb.

Dhanush stared at it without touching it.

Tara paced the room, her hands shaking.

Krish had brought it after their last meeting—a sample taken from Arjun's old toothbrush and an old piece of Sameera's hairbrush Kanika had swiped years ago.

"I don't want to read it," Dhanush muttered.

"You need to," Tara said gently.

He picked it up, unfolded the envelope.

And stared.

Probability of Maternity Match: 99.87%

Sameera Mehta — Biological Mother of Arjun Mehta.

Dhanush dropped the paper like it was on fire.

"She lied to all of us," he whispered.

Tara nodded. "She raised you while hiding him. Split her love. Her empire. Her lies."

"She made me believe I was her only heir."

"You weren't," Tara said. "You were her shield. Arjun was her secret."

Later that day, they brought the results to Dilip.

He was already waiting, with a deeper twist.

"There's something else. About the father."

He handed over an old newspaper clipping.

Justice Rajnath Awasthi found dead in farmhouse. Heart attack suspected.

The article was bland. Clean.

But Dilip added, "I traced a hospital record. A witness had mentioned bruising. Blunt trauma."

Tara's eyes widened.

"He didn't die naturally."

"No. He was killed. And his will was rewritten weeks after."

"And Arjun was his son," Dhanush murmured.

"Which means..." Dilip began.

"...he was supposed to inherit the Awasthi legacy," Tara finished. "And the truth."

They were uncovering not just a murder—but a hidden dynasty.

A shadow empire built on erasure.

And Arjun was supposed to burn it all down.

XXXI

The Circle's Reach

The documents recovered from the Yamuna drive were extensive.

Files. Phone logs. Blacklisted payments.

But one stood out: "Internal Log: T.C. - Confidential Nodes"

It was a list.

One retired General.

Two sitting judges.

A Cabinet Minister.

Three former law enforcement officials.

At the center of the web: Sameera Mehta.

Tara stared at the list.

"The Circle is real."

Dilip nodded. "And bigger than any of us imagined."

But the confirmation came a few days later.

Tara and Dilip were driving back from a journalist's office in Noida when the brakes failed.

The car spun twice before slamming into a divider.

They were lucky to survive.

But it wasn't an accident.

The mechanic confirmed: brake fluid had been drained.

Someone wanted them gone.

Rai came to visit them that night.

He looked older. More tired. And something in his eyes was different, haunted.

"I need to talk," he said quietly.

They led him into the living room. No lights. Just candle glow and static tension.

Rai sat down and said the words they'd suspected but dreaded:

"I was told to stall the case ten years ago."

"By whom?" Tara asked, her voice barely above a whisper.

"A minister. One of Sameera's allies. He said if I kept it buried, I'd be promoted."

"You let Arjun die," Dhanush said flatly.

Rai didn't respond.

Instead, he pulled a sealed envelope from his coat.

"Before he died, Arjun sent me this. I never opened it. I was afraid."

He placed it on the table.

Tara stared at it like it was radioactive.

Written in Arjun's handwriting, across the front:

"Only open if you're ready to know everything."

XXXII

The True Inheritance

The envelope felt heavier than it should have.

Tara opened it slowly, reverently, as if Arjun's voice might spill out between the folds.

Inside was a handwritten letter, faint, uneven in tone.

"If you're reading this, it means I didn't make it. And if I didn't, it wasn't because of money. It was because I finally saw the blueprint. Not just of my family. But of what they've built."

"The 1500 crore estate is a front. The Mehta legacy is a laundering channel for government contracts. From Project Vahana to offshore smuggling to arms supplied to shadow militias."

"Sameera didn't build it. She inherited it. From my father."

"And that money? It was never about me. It was a key. Whoever owns it... controls The Circle."

Tara blinked hard. Dhanush read over her shoulder, stunned.

Dilip's voice was low.

"He knew."

A second slip fell out of the envelope, a notarized file.

Arjun's real will.

It had been countersigned and was ready to be filed the day after his death.

In it, he didn't just name Dhanush the heir.

He appointed Tara Sharma as the legal executor of the Mehta and Awasthi estates.

And with that came access to every hidden document, every account, every ledger, and the ability to destroy The Circle.

Dilip exhaled. "They killed him for this."

Tara whispered, "And now... they'll come for me."

That night, they activated the dead man's protocol.

Multiple data drops, off-site secure backups, and cloud leaks scheduled via VPN.

It was the only way to survive what came next.

XXXIII
Kanika Returns

The email was short.

"One-time link. Secure. Open now."

The video feed opened into a dim, flickering background. A single lamp cast soft light on a familiar face.

Kanika.

Her hair was shorter, darker. She wore glasses. Her voice was lower than Tara remembered, like years in hiding had scraped the brightness from her soul.

"I knew they'd come for me. That's why I ran. But I couldn't stay silent anymore."

She looked straight into the lens.

"Arjun wasn't the first. And he won't be the last unless you take this to the end."

She uploaded a digital locker key.

"It contains a file named 'Vault 7.' It has all their names. All their deals. The whole ecosystem."

Kanika leaned closer.

"Sameera may have been the Queen. But there's still a King out there. Someone Arjun didn't even know."

The screen glitched.

Then her final words:

"Be ready. Because this story doesn't end with justice. It ends with someone else dying."

The screen cut to black.

Tara sat frozen, fists clenched.

Dhanush asked quietly, "Do we open the file?"

Tara nodded once.

And clicked.

The Final Confession

The file took three minutes to decrypt. Three minutes that felt like three hours.

Tara, Dhanush, Dilip, and Aseem sat in total silence, eyes locked to the screen, breath held. When it finally opened, it revealed a neatly organized archive with one headline file:

"Arjun_Final_Video_Log.mp4"

Tara's hand hovered over the mouse.

Then she clicked.

The screen flickered. And there he was.

Arjun Mehta.

Alive. Speaking from the past.

His face was thinner, his eyes sharper. There was weariness in his smile, but fire in his voice.

"If you're watching this, you already know too much."

"I've spent two years digging through my family's rot. It started with Sameera. But it didn't end there."

"The Circle is not just a business cartel. It's a political machine. A shadow state. And I'm the unfortunate legacy of both bloodlines, Mehta and Awasthi."

He paused. His hand trembled slightly.

"My father, Justice Rajnath Awasthi, didn't just sit on the judiciary. He built the mechanism to shield the corrupt elite. He was one of them."

"And my mother, Sameera... she was the enforcer. The fixer. She used me as leverage. As a placeholder until she could wipe the board clean."

"But here's the real twist."

Arjun leaned forward.

His voice dropped to a whisper.

"There's a name no one's said. Someone who never appeared in any file. Never raised suspicion. Never got their hands dirty."

"Dhritirashtra Rai."

Tara's blood went cold.

"He wasn't just the cop assigned to investigate my death. He was planted. Ten years ago. He knew everything."

"He saw me hand Kanika the drive. And he gave Sameera the go-ahead to kill me."

Tara stared at the screen, mouth open.

"And if you're watching this, he's still walking free."

Rai stood outside the safe house, gun tucked in his coat.

His phone buzzed.

One line from a blocked number: "They opened it."

He sighed. "Then it's time."

Inside, Dhanush stood up, white as ash.

"I trusted him," he muttered.

Tara turned, her face stone.

"No more trusting. We burn them all."

Kanika's full archive — "Vault 7" — revealed thousands of documents: smuggled voting records, bribes, murder-for-hire transcripts, even hacked therapy logs of political dissidents.

And there, in the middle, a list labeled "Current Assets" — under the Intelligence Bureau.

Among them: Rai, D. – Active, Clearance Level Black.

Dilip paced the room.

"This is bigger than we imagined."

"We can't release it all at once," Aseem warned. "They'll discredit it. Or worse, erase it."

Tara stared at the final folder.

"Publish_If_I'm_Dead"

Her fingers hovered.

Then clicked.

And the upload began.

XXXV
Truth Kills

The media storm hit like a bomb.

Within 24 hours, the files were everywhere.

Newsrooms. Telegram groups. Leaked to Reddit. Uploaded to academic servers. Mirrored across anonymous global forums.

#MehtaTruth trended for days.

Sameera's empire shattered.

Her assets frozen. Her known properties seized.

And then came the suicides.

A bureaucrat in Mumbai.

A general in Pune.

An ex-judge in Delhi.

Rai disappeared.

Gone.

Vanished into the wind.

But one video surfaced — grainy CCTV — of Rai boarding a freighter ship with a forged diplomatic pass.

Tara watched it twice.

He looked back, just once.

Almost like he knew she'd be watching.

Dhanush received the legal documents confirming full control of the estate.

But he didn't celebrate.

He signed most of it into public trust.

"Let it help fix what we let rot," he said quietly.

Tara kept a small apartment. No guards. No staff. Just peace.

Kanika sent one final message.

"Don't contact me. You did enough. Live."

Six months later.

Tara received a brown envelope in the mail.

No stamp. No address.

Inside, a letter in Arjun's handwriting.

Dated three weeks after his official death.

"I'm sorry I lied. I'm sorry I let you think I died without telling you everything."

"The truth is — part of me had to die to let you live."

"You'll never know everything. But you knew enough to burn it down."

"And for that... I love you."

No signature.

Just the Mehta seal.

Embossed in gold.

Tara stared out her window, hand over her heart.

The world had changed.

But not all ghosts stay buried.

Some leave letters.

Others leave legends.

Thank You To The Reader

Thank you.

Thank you for opening this book. For following every twist, questioning every motive, and holding space for complex characters who weren't always right, but were always real.

In choosing to spend your time with Phones, Lies & Bloodlines, you allowed these voices to echo, these secrets to matter. Whether you felt rage, heartbreak, relief, or revelation, I'm honored that this story became part of your world, even briefly.

If it stayed with you, I hope you'll tell someone. Whisper the title. Recommend it to a friend. Or leave a review that helps other curious readers find their way here.

Until we meet again, in pages or elsewhere, stay sharp, stay kind, and keep seeking the truth.

With deep gratitude,
Divija Shekhawat